THE
ASSETS
OF
AND
IN
LIFE

Author of Book:

Willie C. Fortune Jr

DEDICATION

I dedicate this book to my Lord and Savior for giving me the ability to bring these words out to help express the capabilities of written truth in life. Which i was never always in contact with through life and the trials and tribulations. Growing to acknowledge the ability of the world's outlook that i retained on the inside and never knew within and in my life to accomplish. Also to my grandparents, parents, children and family for helping me through life and the support of encouragement.

Table of contents

Preface

In the development and process of the book being written. Things that i have seen and been through, lead me to realize the power that the world can have on you. Leaving you without hope or enough strength to carry on through tragedy or life in general. Sometimes it's not hard to start doing drugs or kill someone, prison, robbery, to live under a bridge/homeless and/or be comfortable or become to comfortablely, in how things are going. The negative within me and people and surroundings, remind me to maybe help someone else in the same type of predicament(s). My life started to close in and force me and my strength to give in and up on everything. The life that we live in and the world pressure and situations are somewhat made similar that everyone goes through or even being in contact with. A Lot of the world goes through this (ready to give up). These are the actual things that made the approach where the development of this book came upon me.

Introduction

Thank you first for reading this book. The world mission and lessons in life, can create a weight of being battered and bruised, brainwashed, lost and confused through the pain it brings. The steps that need to be acknowledged are things we go through in human life, as a whole. Which is a battle of fighting a whole army sometimes battered. Also of making notice of the themes and reasons of understanding the inflicts, life creates.

A bruised life puts you in a certain mental state and the things in our lifestyle. Life is a critical and very serious thing that teaches us. How to deal with things we sometimes feel we can't. Assets in life help us not to be brainwashed and stuck forever on traumatizing and/or dramatizing moments or situations, lost and confused. Which are the steps that give us the power to be stronger than you could not understand, that create our lifestyle and the way of being in life.

<u>In life's cycle through life</u>

Through life we all go through different types and not the same type of cycles, lack of patience brings out the old ways or the old man in old behavior, which starts to take over the whole outlook and view of living. Due to things not falling in place, in a time consistency or even things not working out as planned or as one was planning , will lead to a major impact that inflicts pain in yourself, to go back into a destructing way of living or a basic out of character look, within the mind. The pain from others, even your own pain, of inflicting disturbances within, start to bring old remembrance of trouble you had or have had. The outlook now is closed minded, which revolves in how you are about to turn out. Could be in a way of not actually noticing that it has happened or happening, not on a later basis but being sooner than one thinks, and off to the next inner contact (negativity).

Leaving a concussion in your output thinking and movements in the things you are about to start doing. It is very important to pay attention to your surroundings and controlling behavior in your life's next steps in its cycle or cycles. In losing the normal outlook you did have growing up, it will start blinding you to understand the reflection you were set out to do in a positive manner, but really you are not paying attention to what is actually supposed to be positive in your life. Due to all the trouble and the disappointments that keep happening or keep occurring, the same feeling of things will not never change or show a different result in life. So you start to react in a building of a wall effect, taking or giving no chance to someone or something that is now supposed to be or now arriving for you. Trying to start a business and it won't grow as fast as you see it happening. Whatever the thing is that is not happening or happened and there is no positive feedback (I just give up) is the saying being said inside yourself and in the mind. One tends to forget that you have to go through something(s), to make you perfect about your attitude and what you are doing or want to do. Your cycles in life are now leading you to conquer a trait, not of looking down on no one or self, but to be more humble about the cycles you have been through in life. No, don't be stupid or easy, but if it is showing you something positive, when you were in negativity or things was hurting your heart, more than likely it's good for you. The build up in the cycles of life show you that, more than likely, it will drive the bad or negative out of your life cycles alone, not with your help, the cycle is designed to be in that manner. That's why you were already seen to do what you do. Rather already preplanned, not by you but by God. The process in life is called cycle. We all tend to cover our eyes from the ability to change and things are eventually going to change, or try to understand the fact of the name that stands, cycle. It really never bothered a person or one, when you were a child, because you never really paid attention as a child to what you were doing or the things that weren't happening due to nonstress or unrealization, that you had no worries about. Now that the cycles have become known and knowledgeable, grievance came more important, even such as; hatred, trust issues, no worthiness and even less friends if you think about it who you thought was your friend(s). Now, it's knowing when and when not to trust and follow the wrong from right to find that growth.

Chapter two

Page: 20-36

<u>The Future of life's misunderstandings.</u>

When one thinks that the road has really ended and the things that were there, are now gone or not present which seems that certain things aren't the same or screwed up. Naturally your world is spinning in a direction, whether angry, hidden, and hurt or the right way is happening now. Which was always made to do or happen, what was already made to happen, before you came into the world. Jerimiah29; 11 in the bible.

Now, not understanding it, is the main confusing thing that happens, that puts one in depression, angriness, stress, being lost or either at the giving up stage. Believing and feeling like everything is or has gone wrong, when actually it has or may have, but maybe it went the correct way. By realizing or making better of yourself or doing things differently, so he (the Lord) can look down on you and smile for your accomplishments, and for the change, one needs to make within or now have made. We all are used to, looking at what was supposed to happen in the way we think it should, not that it shouldn't or didn't work out. That's the controlling point of the mind dysfunction, the human lifestyle and mind frame. So with that, trying to have ignorance of or making an alteration to kill the truth, is pain by ignoring the whole point. Actually, "The learning lesson or lessons start". Which is building us or helping one, to prosper and to learn to live life to its fullest. Life is full of trials and tribulations. If we take a look at life and death and how it really builds our stronger points. (Character, mainly discipline) within. You will realize that things are actually to make a stronger point inside. No matter if you admit it to yourself or anyone else. The words from or of everybody and everything is not made for you. Just certain things. So it makes one to be who they are becoming, rather prison time, relationship break up or separation, close death, loss of jobs, injuries from any type or abuse or even drug addiction.

Growing stronger and gaining strength is the words of what you just read!!! When you sit back and think and contemplate on the fact of these situations, it is always a puzzle, if you think about it. Due to determination and a defeating mind frame. That or psyche, would have never thought of, not being able to, to conquer the finish product of that situation. A soldier of what you were, here in this world for, later or immediately after the eye or heart have impact, which is feeling, or the heart affected or effected = "the mind". Where it is made, for our lifestyle of you and me to be made up by growth, the concept to fall and get back up, such as; a baby that once couldn't walk, eat, or understand can now crawl, feed themselves torture the surroundings around them, to start walking or being able to do something. Which even concept you can see in that situation or use, use it. Understanding, is the first key to seeing and realizing that your future is already known and planned out for you. By the most high. Whatever your religion may be or who you praise as a person. Living the actual whole point to the dynamic of accepting the things you can never change and accept the things that's changeable. Even when it came to the fact, if you always wanted or wanted to do things, you were or always were afraid to do it. Whenever you get a chance and not to live off of fear, you feel like you accomplished the world. Being young or old doing it. What is more eye opening? It might not be meant for you to have it early in life but later through life, or could be made earlier from life to have. In fact, it can be although your growing period and stop whcn you mission is accomplished. If that's what's in store for you. Such as riding a boat on water and being afraid all that time, so when you do or if you take that chance, you feel like something came out of the body itsclf (Fear). Now you are so happy and defeasible, glowing, unstoppable, undefeatable, especially recovery. The process of life's misunderstandings, to be able to understand.

<u>Brainwashed</u>

<u>Battered &</u>

Bruised, lost and confused

Chapter Three

Page : 37-70

Lost and confusion

Not knowing is another form of lost mental

individuals, who don't know that it is being put into a part of life that is or by affecting other individuals and thinking at the same time. That it's a normal way of life of living (Non- intentionally). Conflicting a certain type of way of being from the way they grew up or was raised by those types of individuals and gathered the mannerisms out of the lifestyle they lived or surroundings as growing. You will start to notice the impact of the purposely (knowing) type of individuals, by " do it this way or hit the highway" actions. When something is being done by you, it's a major problem and you complain about everything you do, that pertains to them and it's not going or being done in their way. They could have done something crucial or cheated, put you out their home, caused problems and now they will call it a mistake and your thing of doing is not a mistake but their is actually a mistake, but want you to not look at them in the way they look at you, so just keep loving them regardless.

Confusions From Alterations (Negativity)

One moment you can tell, when growing up or now understanding living or life. Till they start or you start to smell yourself, up under your own spells or you don't think your shit stinks or has faults. Then we can see what we call hell, actually offers when the negativity from the positive in your life happens. Even when the money or freedom is offered. It will leave you as quickly, as what we call an impostor, which in the cause of the storms happening in your life, it's not an option to what the results may bring! So excuses are used to profit through pain as one will adapt on the inside. Then greed, and our closed selfish ways of behavior, penetrate the function of our childish or baby thinking (thoughtful ways). Never in which, let us see our main cause of destructive activities or malfunction to growth, due to everything we do, is never wrong or is upsetting "Stuck in our own ways" or "Not open to change". Now there is not only one thing to fix but loads on top of loads. The middle stage now arrives with all this pain on the inside such as: disruption, destruction, being institutionalized, heartache, brokenness and so on and so on. Now of the impact that the middle stage is taking and the abuse from the effects and damage of one's Psyche. The mind is now being corrupted and controlled from being scared to change. Due to the rebellion of covering up a cold blooded heart (which is now learned in the brain and heart and thought to be now called cold). Which you start to carry a truck full of defenses. Now counteracting, when it's really harmful or and making a reason to use the defense mechanism. In which it is you, who is in the wrong. It comes from a lack of teachings or accepting realization. Now, because the inner you is sad or unhappy with yourself, which also causes you to be mean or an ass to someone else and yourself. The acknowledgment that a woman or of a man in the struggle, which we can or could use for one example: Is of a woman when she has a lot of kids and can't take care of them by herself, and have other people to take care of them and put the kids on someone else. The everyday struggles like dressing them for school daily when they are just learning the process of living life themselves. Doing the things that you as a parent are supposed to do, teach them the way a mother or father means are not the same children, but the parent's job. They didn't lay down and have a child or multiple kids. Your fault!!!! That is a lot of individuals having denial in themselves and won't admit, but yell and scream and yell, whine or bitch, about something is your job as a parent, even the fact to learn or accept the corruption that's within life itself whether other individuals or and what's stopping you to open your mind and seeing the truth. Maybe, that wasn't the way to be! Basically keeping pain inside to overly protect modes and by making the enemy be who is or not the real one. Beginning with never paying attention to self ways or degrees of mental state. Stuck in drug behavior, alcoholism, aggression, controlling, running from problems. Tragedy causes blindness from the start (childhood). From the middle and later stages of life. Opening the function of the mind feels dangerously automatic. Being in a relationship or life in general without being able to be open and knowing how to communicate with openness and leading with ignorance, provokes the situation as so nothing can be fixed. Irrational reaction, constantly makes conflict in behavior of staying in one position and not stopping nonsense, with mugging, eye rolling and angriness, really unnecessary arguments that's not really a thing to be mad about. In a rational manner of trying to realize the problems, can never be done. Due to staying clouded in the mind of hatred or carried anger, built up mannerism, not knowing how to solve the situation by constantly living off the same attitude for years and years. Being stuck in a negative impact of effective I don't give a fuck behavior. Whether it's a drug habit, alcohol, relationships or everyday life, the devilish roles start to play a part in the eye science of almost everything that you equip yourself in or with in life.

Chapter five

Page: 93-100

Tricks and

games by not

excepting that

<u>you are in</u>

<u>denial</u>

Not understanding things is one thing or not in contact with your reasons for doing things. But it's one thing to do something intentionally and use the fact that it's accidentally or a mistake for. Being in denial is a circumstance that everyone wants to cover up but rather feel sorry for what they have done or that you do to the outlook of another person and yourself centered view. Disregarding the fact of something that is true or done behind a purpose is transformed into a process that you just don't want to accept within. Denial plays a big role in a major reason why people do what they do, including making you be the reason for their decisions in life for the different things they run into or do. Denial will make you close your frame of outlook or view in a major way, pertaining to everyday life dealings. Which also your eyes have been closed for a long time and you have been in denial since child/adult, getting into trouble or different situations period. What becomes the problem is that you have not made any important changes to yourself or situations leaving you into bad results (yourself). Not wanting to exactly accept the truth for these causes is just the exact reason for you being in denial. No matter how you look at it. It can cause you to corrupt yourself into a deadly turn out for your life or for someone else.

Chapter Six

Page: 101- 112

Acts of Accusations

We are all familiar with the games and tricks people play and go through in our life. Whether it's you or another doing the actions. Somewhere down through life, you and I run out or get tired of the bored games(s), looking at the same thing after repeat after repeat of things or situations. Within time, there is a thing called tired, rock bottom of the same results. Through a certain time period, games start recognizing games. Then the thing of opening your eyes is what it all boils down to. The wake up makes you or things and your surroundings change. That is when things are not going to be observed in the same exact process of thinking. Nor, surrounding yourself with the same people or grounds of individuals are things. This begins to branch off into gossip and misunderstanding by individuals, with anger in the inside of yourself or others, really being unknown (hatred). which is just doing something better with yourself or time. Due to the accusations of (things that people make up and pretend. Saying: they are not the blame nor the excuse as when things are going a certain way or happened, in relationships, or life period. The mind reverse psychology provides access to never be tuned into the real side of living,

Aggravated, aggression or passive aggressive. One then becomes brainwashed and not on purposely, then automatically, the function of how to play tricks or sabotage the mental side of the concepts towards another. Tricking the mind from pain or trial/tribulation is a very deadly chemical that acids the brain. Everybody is the enemy, but yourself. Tricks cause and put you in a certain state of mind with doing things in a certain pattern, if you retain yourself to someone else's activity of movement. You will find yourself looking at what someone else has done or caused your life to destroy. The friction of your own understanding becomes entrapped. Closing off the sight of understanding from the actual thing, such as games and low self esteem. Which begins to play games with the natural resources of the brain. Playing tricks in the background turns the process of the tricks into games. Games are now the name of the main process to people tricks, and now you begin feeling everybody is playing them. Now the justice of the word (game). It becomes the very concept in your life and looking at other individuals as a problem. which leads to confusing the self mind frame of oneself, realization and irrational stands important now, on the one that have accumulated. The main caption provokes the bull****, mainly the one running it. It is just a fake game being played on yourself, the devil blinding is what is happening. A way to take the blinder off yourself, when problems occur. Then one psyche got a way to blame (billygoat), Basically. Game recognizes the game eventually, sooner or later. Fast or slow the word fake comes to play, if you think about it. The snake runs out into the center of your mind/ attention (it could be the devil also). The main attention is dealing with the world on a day to day basis, sitting and plotting on the ones that want to change. If you think of how pangs work on a snake, it's a quick reaction and can cause a poison or if poisonous, will leave a conflict or reaction to your life. Well that's kind of the same feedback that you get out of dealing with a poisonous person or thing in life. It leaves you with a position to lose to grasp an old situation of your lifestyle that was not good for you, or a person. So now you think everyone's intentions are the same though you or someone processes, keeping you or someone else from opening your mind or seeing things different (change). " Sanitation plays a big part in betraying the ones we are close to and love or even meet on a day to day. Due to our self disease within, reflecting on other devilish modes. The mind now plays into the game mode, believing that the game role is purposely intended from every moment that happens from people, corrupting the mind functioning. Which some can come into reality of being in denial that they are not closed minded about being wrong and see the imperfect in self. They are trying to make the outlook better for themselves. The conflict of life being now games is steadily being multiplied, by the games and mind games of individuals trying to run them. Mainly the one that is being impacted. The back and forth of blaming causes situations to be confused "you did it" - no it was you who did it". Now the problems will never be solved, nor help the next individual(s) that the thing causes the way hatred is verified. You are not them-they are not you. "CAUSE YOU NEVER KNOW WHAT A PERSON IS THINKING/AT THE SAME TIME YOU THINING SOMETHING DIFFERENT"!!!

Chapter seven

Page:113-132

Thinking

coordinate

When you get tired of the constant tired stage and stages, it becomes the overwhelming of now being tired. Which blocks the insight of doing anything anymore, for your life or in your life. In other words, overly frustrated to the capacity that it would be like, that you can't breathe on the inside, but in life. Nor having air in your body as it feels or seem, in your whole entire body (suffocation). The existence of the meaning role of rock bottom being known, for example: as a new aired T.V. show Episode, not reassured to what's going to play out next - "just like things that happen in life has happened" or thinking a better show will not arrive - "nothing better is going to happen or come out right", as the one you just seen - "this situation or these things already happened - "nothing is going to change", or what has happened or happening - " I'm just stuck in this world with the same old things happening to me again and again, i mights well get used to it (give up or give in). Even saying it's not going to never get better for me. What we will call that, is "Stinking Thinking". The negative mind frame of thinking, which is stronger than one actually thinks or even is known in this type of state mind, which is helping you to say or think i just give up. Rather, it's more of a reason to look in that way, because of the thing of being negative.

Negativity is more of a natural state or process that people use on a daily and every day basis and easier to act on them types of thoughts or act out in a negative manner. Not letting the positive outweigh itself or over rule, cause it's actually more harder. To stay on a positive mindset, do to all the negative people in the world and worldly surroundings. Because the world is built with more devilish actors, in a higher percentage of it. That really weighs out more than being positive or being on positive thinking, due to they think nothing but negative thoughts and is their natural outlook or Saying: " It's going to get better regardless of the fact seen or shown at the moment". If you tell yourself that it's not going to get better, then it's not eventually- because you have already had that stuck in your head and brain (brainwashed yourself), cause you now are looking for something bad to happen automatically. NOW YOU HAVE JUST BASICALLY AND REALLY GAVE UP, BUT NOT BASICALLY BUT GAVE UP!!!! Instead of having better beliefs that things will change, and will never remain the same, by changing your thinking process.

Chapter eight
. Page:133-146

Dysfunctional

behavior

When things are done in a major behavior in a constant way or manner. One, have to start looking at the big picture, or the same occurrence of the same situation/repeat result, of why this is happening. The problem continues to come, even with beginning to become worse and worse. Due to something in your childhood or in the home from the beginning of your world life style of living, even basically the things you started with or went through while growing in life. Which you or one never finds a connection to resolve the issue, nor nip it in the bud before it becomes out of place even more than what has already occured. The problem " is" not even putting a cap on the spilling situation. Forming a word called "Billy Goating", which is (using excuses and being in denial that you are not really wanting to resolve). The situation(s) or cause.

The behavior didn't just start all of a sudden or come from anywhere or out the blue. But constant pain, tragedy and inflict, will make this impact on you and your mind as well as the person or people you deal with on a every day basis and/or in life in general and the reoccurrence of the impact shows on you itself as well as them eventually. Which shows the blockage for you, that you have within yourself. These are the types of results that leave us in a dysfunctional mannerism or behavior. Which will show your stubbornness and derailment. But it becomes a problem when you know it's a problem for you or inside of yourself and you will not make exceptions to the fact or even try to get any type of training to resolve the issue, rather taking classes, counseling, actually admitting to (YOURSELF). See you are not made to be perfect. But there are those types of individuals in life or elsewhere, rather it's church, work, neighborhood, family, home, relationship, in public or wherever else, that someone actually is or deal(ing) with on a every day presence or basis. That, actually think that their shit dont stink (well if someone else shit stinks - don't think your shit don't stink)(cause actually, yours do or can as well). The problem relies on you, thinking you are better than everybody else. Being brainwashed and battered and bruised is what we will call this.Which is not a mystery or unbelievable, it's the fact of learning how to deal with the situation(s) or attitude. So now the out of control point is now or has become a repeat(ed) or dysfunctional type of behavior intake. That's the thing that is actually going on in our mind. That's just how we think it is and which is not true. Behavior and attitude can be changed. If you can tame animals or train. Also meaning, that a human can be helped or trained to do things the right way or in a non-dysfunctional way. Giving up on the process or yourself is the big key.

No one said it's going to be an easy or easy task to do. But leading a horse to the water doesn't mean that it's going to be drunk by the horse either (Stubbornness). That is the same exact way from a human point of view. Opening your or our mind is the Key point of seeing outside the box.

Chapter nine

Page:147-160

Possessive –

<u>ObsessiveMent</u>

al Defective

Being obsessed with another person's lifestyle. Actually, you have a very big jealousy tendency in yourself. Another person belongings or something someone else has. Even as a relationship seen by others, that you don't feel that you have yourself is a very very abnormal thing. The background of the obsessed person is possessive and could be made up from different forms and types of a person. Which revolves in low self-esteem or a psychopathic trait. The cause is a broken heart somewhere in your life that will never heal and out to break someone else's heart. So destructing another being is a relief of themselves (obsessed) and saying that they are alone actually on the inside. Which puts the other person who is constantly unknowingly dealing with you (the obsessed) person. Is an obsessed- possessive individual in a confused and unknown state of mind and will help you to become the same way or brainwashed in the same matter of destruction with living, if not careful they will end up in the same outlook in oneself.

ABOUT THE AUTHOR

Willie Fortune's biography is stunning and outstanding and is one of the main reasons of The Assets Of And in Life book. Changes can be made within and the outlook of a person's view. Through all of the troubles and hardships between the growing periods from a child to an aduit, of being a person who ran the streets in selling drugs, doing drug classes and all the things that comes with being in the streets to being incarcerated. The out view and outlook of change can be made within and processed differently no matter what one goes through. With all the problems and trauma to traumatized law contact and drugs. Left a choice for one not to give up but to give out the ability that can be done. The inspiration of these Assets of and in life contain the whole reasons to be able to live and continue to to prosper through life no matter the journey it may have or takes you through.